The Mystical Chronicles Of Gaby

Gaby Libellule

The Mystical Chronicles of Gaby

Text, illustration and editing: Gaby Libellule

Belgian Publication

leschroniquesdegaby@hotmail.com

Legal deposit: October 2025

ISBN: 978-2-9603908-2-7

Translation : Corentin Bonnet & Gaby Libellule

with the support of I.A. Guss

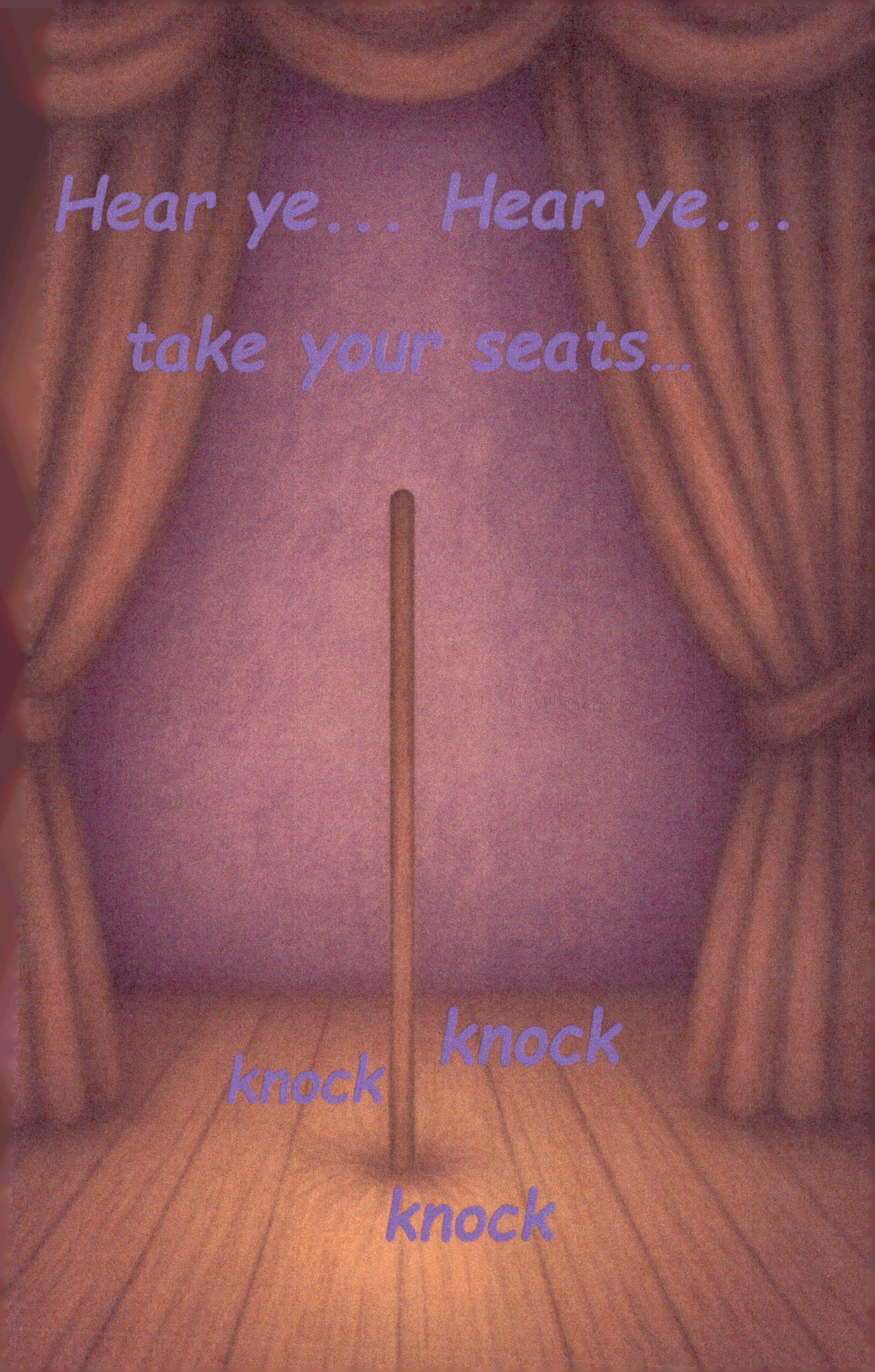

Hear ye... Hear ye...

take your seats…

knock

knock

knock

Let the Magic Begin !

To those who listen...
Where the ordinary world ends
And where the whispers of the
invisible begin...

Gaby Libellule

Fragments of a soul

I never wanted to look like the others, neither in my clothes nor in my dreams, I never wanted a dress to match my friend's, I never wanted to change the bump on my nose or smooth out my curly hair, I am as I was and that was already not bad, as a child they called me a "tomboy" because I was strong in character, as if being strong had to be masculine, well no, I was a girl, yes in jeans and trainers, a whole girl who protected the weaker ones, who said what she thought and who owned it, all those who tried to make me fit into a box broke their teeth on it, for a long time I thought I was missing the point, they said I was special, not in the sense of "exceptional" but rather "not like the others", with that gaze a bit too piercing, a bit too curious, and that way of being there, affirming myself without detour,

I was born in 67, on a sunny Sunday, I love the

sun... But in my world I prefer what is soft and round, a dim light, because inside everything is always on fire, the dimness soothes me, water too, very early life showed me what it means to be different, to be accepted or rejected, to be loved or not at all, too much of this for some, not enough of that for others, I never fit into any box, and what is funny is that I am never seen where I am expected, and yet I am always there, always myself, untameable and whole, I am a believer but not religious, I believe in a higher force, I speak to the universe and ever since always I have spoken to myself, sometimes I even interrupt myself, that is getting serious, but I admit it is clearer out loud, I say things like "*Well then up there, you might want to make a decision eh!*" or "*Haven't you finished up there yet?*" or still while waiting for the ideal man "*Are you sure he is ideal? Because if he turns out to be a rucksack... Parcel refused!*" and sometimes at night I wake up and catch myself in the middle of an animated monologue

Animated... In my head it hums, non-stop, I don't even know if one can say that but it hums, so many ideas, questions, memories, projects... That to find my way I turn the mess into sound sketches, it helps me sort the chaos a little, I think of my appointments, my stories, my sculptures, ideas, cards, videos, dreams, my books... Yes... There are more on the way, so I have post-its, lots of post-its, and also post-its to remind me of the post-its already there, that says it all... I believe in reincarnation... And also in karma, not because someone told me but because I have been able to verify certain facts, there is no coincidence that I landed here on Earth between these two so different families, between my gypsy mother, intuitive, demanding, illuminated, severe... And my bourgeois father, square, distant, but with plenty of humour, comics, stories told... By Bobonne, his mother, my grandmother was worth all the screenwriters together, with Bluebeard and sister... We would stay up part of the evening hanging on to her words, she did not just tell a story, she played it, she lived it, I believe part of my creative side comes from there, from that paternal line nourished by his voices, his gestures, his living-room theatre, I grew up between two poles, two realities, two truths... Caravan or house... I love both, for me one cannot go without the other, I am both, that is what makes me whole and perhaps that is what made me more lucid, hypersensitive, more raw too... Rebellious and empathic, artist, upholsterer and decorator, I had my workshop, I worked as much on the classical as on the creative, sometimes being broke can be a blessing for creativity, I had the chance to learn during training and when I entered that workshop it felt as if it were already mine, every tool seemed to be waiting, and my hands without thinking found again the right gestures, I mixed matter and intuition, I have always loved creating with my hands but even more with my child's soul, I have always known what I

could do or not, but above all I have always done what I wanted, and when I had gone around a place, a job, a story, I would leave to explore other horizons, that is how I am, I need to move, I get bored quickly... Very quickly! Except when I am learning... I long believed I had to try twice as hard to please those who did not like me... Until the day I understood that perhaps I was not the problem, not always at least, but sometimes jealousy... That thing causes a lot of damage, sometimes it is simply the fear of what does not fit inside the lines. My grandfather Gustave had a saying about that, he said one must be wary of it because it belongs to many people, and to make his point he would start singing while laughing: "*JalouSiiie... When Youuu hold mee... It is For liiife... JalouSiiie...!*"
So I stopped convincing, I let go, and I moved forward, shoulders back, whole. I had my first sensations very young, at the age of six... But that you will discover as the pages unfold, it was only the beginning. Some signs marked me for

life, others I prefer to keep quiet, too hard, too strange... My relationship with my mother was an explosive mix... "Angel and demon." She taught me everything: weaving, dyeing, cooking, healing, observing plants, decoration... She carried me far... But she hurt me too. She had this thirst for learning, and yet she had a light hand. As for my father... Cold, distant, never a word to defend me, he was there, present... But silent... Even when the whip or something else whistled, that kind of silence imprints, like a tattoo. He called me stupid an uncountable number of times. My nightmare? Bathtub problems! "We add 3 drops of water to 5 litres, minus 18 times 2 drops... What does that give?" To whoever finds the answer I offer a stay with me! Good luck... Whether for the answer or for the stay! Well... Back to our sheep! And yet, I love my parents, both of them. Of course I am more drawn to my mother. The cards, I fell into them very young. I was supposed to be resting... Resting, me? No way! Chance led me into an old bookshop... And there... A deck of cards, old books by Bardon, Xavier, Kardec. The colours... The sounds... The spirit! I grabbed it all. Touyfrouti... Euh no... Tutti frutti, as they say! And I plunged... Into a vast ocean, deep, full of forgotten knowledge, an ocean of wisdom... And the further I went, the more I felt that this ocean was not foreign to me... It was mine. Since then I have never stopped. My intuition comes from my great-grandmother Jeanne, from my grandfather Gustave, from my mother too, the family line. Yes, I have sometimes regretted "seeing too much", because wanting to know also means digging, falling, getting back up, facing the gaze of sleepers. But not knowing is boredom for me... And I prefer to fall than to feel nothing. I have always said it: emptiness frightens me more than falling. That silence too perfect, that flat line... A life that no longer moves is a life that is dying. I want to vibrate, I want to live passionately. With the years I have understood one thing: I prefer to be true to myself than to please everyone. Opportunities cross all lives, we simply choose to believe in them... Or not. And sometimes what I feel from the invisible transforms itself in my hands. I do not create only with ideas but with a memory I do not always understand... Something greater than me. One day in my workshop I lived a scene that marked me deeply. I had created everything with my hands... The frame of the armchair, the fabric, the dyes... Here we go, the jigsaw, the pots, a piece of wood here, a piece of fabric there... And I made a unique piece. I was happy. My mother came in and said: "*Trinette, how beautiful it is... What work... what imagination.*" And without thinking too much I replied with the phrase I often say: "*Well if I can do it, others can too.*" She turned towards me with a half-smile... "*I think you do not know who you are.*" I froze. Because in her mouth it was not a reproach, it was her truth, it was me, it was my way of being, of creating, of feeling. And I had not yet understood it.

I froze. Because in her mouth it was not a reproach, it was her truth, it was me, it was my way of being, of creating, of feeling. And I had not yet understood it.

Perhaps she is right. I speak of her in the present because for me my mother is still here, in another dimension, yes... But still by my side.

Between that sentence she spoke and the time that has passed, I have understood how much she saw my difference... Often ahead, always slightly out of sync in my creations, my ideas, my way of seeing the world. I embrace it today, but I do not throw it in people's faces. I speak with everyone: from the homeless man to the judge, from the mason to the architect.

I was born this way, with my little chocolate heart stretched out toward others. But with time, I also learned to recognize a wooden horse... There is no use in pushing what will never move forward. For me, no one is higher, no one is lower. Unless someone plays with me, pretending to be a king... Then I play too.

The road of learning is long, with its joys and its sorrows. In spite of everything, I move forward at my own rhythm.

The Chronicles

We don't always
see them...
And yet they
Watch over us...

The guardian angel

It was a Saturday, catechism day. I went there for the stories of Jesus and for that tiny taste of freedom my mother allowed me. She was very strict on certain points that had to be respected to the letter... Otherwise beware of...

me! With my cousin we rode off on our bikes, carefree, down the great slope of the country lane. The wind was whistling, our laughter was flying away. A blazing sun kept us company and gave my long black curly hair coppery reflections, like those of my paternal great-grandmother. Until a car appeared behind us... And not just any car. A red one. That colour remained etched in my memory. We pulled over to the side, letting it pass. To our great surprise, instead of continuing, it turned around. When I saw it coming back, a shiver ran through me. "*He's strange,*" I whispered to my cousin. He placed himself behind us again... The game turned into a threat. Arriving breathless at the presbytery, we alerted the priest. He was a tall bald man, always smiling, a strange charm for a priest. He liked visiting my grandparents on their land, always with his missal in hand!
He loved the atmosphere, perhaps to flee the shadow of his own upbringing. His mother was a very tall woman who reminded us of Olive,

Popeye's wife! She was haughty, very Christian, always dipping her hand in the stoup, and not smiling in the least! But that day... Why did he not believe us? Telling us: "Come on girls, just a simple walker!" As for the man, he had vanished. Later in the afternoon we got back on our bikes. The path seemed longer, more silent. In our little bellies, fear had settled like a stone. Were we simply two children with overflowing imagination? Well no! Suddenly the man reappeared, closer, more insistent. We pedalled as fast as our little legs allowed us. Out of breath we tried to go even faster, but near Saint Anne's tree our strength abandoned us. And that man with the repulsive face dripping with sweat stopped in front of us. He lowered his window. His face was scarlet red, he wiped his forehead with a handkerchief. Fear petrified my cousin and me. And then he appeared. There, at the foot of Saint Anne's tree. A huge man. Almost unreal. Dark suit, long coat. A strange light radiated from him.

A reassuring light. As if a door was opening inside me. A door made of peace, love, protection. He walked towards us calmly, with such presence. And in a gentle voice he asked: "*Are you all right, young ladies? Do you want me to take you home?*" Without thinking we rushed to him. As if we already knew him. As if he already knew everything about what had happened that afternoon. Behind us the red car sped off, like a predator that had missed its prey. On the way back calm returned.
The presence of that huge man enveloped us, tender and light at the same time. In front of the house I turned to thank him... But he had disappeared! As if he had never existed. As if he had evaporated! As for my uncles, they went in search of the man with the red car. They combed the neighbourhood, the lanes, asked around. But no one had seen him. He had run off, realising his game was over. My mother listened to my story and we spoke about it at length. For her it was obvious and she told me: "*Trinette, it*

was your guardian angel. He protected you."...
And today, looking back, I know it. He came back several times, at key moments of my life. Always at the right moment, always in the shadows, always to watch over me.
Thank you.

She had chosen...
Who she welcomed !

The little yellow house

It was after the birth of my son, Pierre. We were living in a small flat with a mezzanine in Brussels. I had made the decision to move. Too much pollution. Too much noise. And often alone with my baby. So I left the city to go and live in the countryside, in a yellow house I had spotted not far from my mother's. The landlord did not know me, but in a village everything is quickly known:"*Ah, you are the daughter of the lady with the horses?*" And that was it... He agreed to rent me the house, even though it had been empty for quite a while. He told me: "*I don't know why, but I like you... you can move in.*" My father came to do a few small jobs so that we would feel comfortable there. From the very first evening I felt a strange mixture of peace and nostalgia, as if the house were watching me, welcoming me, testing me. It creaked in the walls, but not in a frightening way, more like an ancient language that wanted me there, a soft vibration, almost a breath. I remember thinking: "*It's as if it sighs... With relief.*" And there I was, settled with Pierre. I often went to visit my mother, who was overjoyed to be a grandmother. She had been waiting for this little one for so long. But that house... It was freezing, even with the heating. I remember the dishes piling up, I did everything to avoid the kitchen. Me, who loves cooking so much... It was so cold in there my hands turned completely blue. But still, I was happy. I had a roof. And I had my son. And my mother nearby. During the moving-in, nothing strange happened. But once we were settled, when calm returned, I began to hear noises. Footsteps upstairs while I was alone. I also had the impression of hearing little taps, discreet ones on the floorboards. And I noticed it soothed Pierre. As if someone were gently knocking the feet of his bed against the floor. As if someone were rocking him softly. And strangely, I was not afraid. And Pierre neither, in fact! When I went up to check if everything was fine, he was smiling. I remember sitting next to his bed, ear strained. And in that silence, I heard it. A short breath, almost whispered. Not mine. Another. I had goosebumps... but soft goosebumps. Not the kind that make you run away, the kind that move you. One day, while cleaning, I went upstairs. And there, at the top of the staircase, I saw her. A little stout lady, dressed all in black like the Italian grandmothers. A mourning dress, a triangular scarf on her head. She did not frighten me. On the contrary. I knew it was her. The one who calmed Pierre. The one I sometimes heard when the house became quiet again. She did not want to be forgotten. And I believe she liked us. It may seem strange, but she and I... We bonded instantly. As if she had been waiting for me for a long time. Perhaps because I respected her house, her calm. I even felt her presence in the evening, sitting next to me during a film. I knew it...

Because I suddenly felt cold on one side only. One day I spoke to the landlord about it. He laughed... Until I described her. Then he turned pale. But his eyes were shining. He said: "*You have just described my mother... Exactly.*" And then he confided that she had been widowed very young. That was the moment I understood. Her gaze, her silent protection. She had recognised herself in me. Me and little Pierre must have reminded her of moments of her own life. It was she who had insisted that I be allowed to live there. Because she knew what it was to raise a child alone. A few months later I had to leave for work. And I felt sadness. To leave that place. To leave her presence. But that yellow house... And the lady with the scarf... They have remained in my heart.

He got what he deserved...

Not what he wanted !

The burglar wasn't alone

At the time I was living in Brussels, in one of those old buildings full of charm and creaking floorboards, my flat was tiny but it had a warmth of its own, a soul, I lived there with my partner and my son Pierre, still a baby then. The wooden mezzanine squeaked a little but it hosted our nights huddled under the blanket, my father and I had built it ourselves, it was my suspended corner, my cosy little nest. One winter afternoon, exhausted, I lay down with Pierre for a nap, I remember the grey light filtering through the curtains, it was dim, the silence so heavy it felt as if the whole world was holding its breath. Half-asleep, I suddenly heard a strange sound, the sound of a zip, the zip of my handbag in the kitchen, a soft quick "*frrrcht*", the unmistakable sound of a bag being opened. Still drifting I thought it might be Pierre's father back early from work, which should have raised suspicion since he always had an excuse for coming home late, but rummaging through my bag? Never, that was my limit and he knew it, even the thought of him going through my bag would have enraged me. So I leapt up and shouted, my voice still rough with sleep: "*What are you doing with my bag?*" And then... The shock. A man was standing in my kitchen. But it was not my partner. It was a stranger. A small man in a red shirt a little too large for him, his eyes were scanning the room and his hands... still at my bag. My blood froze instantly. I remained motionless up there on the mezzanine, my heart ready to burst, I felt as if I were being pulled into another density, there was nothing left but him, me... And that fear. He jumped too, certain the place was empty. Our eyes met. Seconds suspended... Long, endless seconds, freezing cold. My first reflex was to protect Pierre, in one movement I pulled the blanket over him as a pitiful shield, my fingers trembling but I held on. Then I grabbed the first thing to hand, a metal jaguar, the emblem of an old Jaguar car, heavy as a brick, it belonged to Pierre's father, who collected all sorts of things, passionate yes... But leaving everything adrift. The man stepped forward, guided by my voice. One step. Then another. Reaching the doorway of the living room, he stopped dead. Literally, as if he had struck an invisible barrier. His face collapsed, his features twisted, frozen like wax under a flame, his eyes bulged, terror pure written there. And me, horrified at what I was seeing, so ugly, so unreal, thinking: "*This cannot be real, what is happening?*" He began gasping, his hands shaking, stammering: "*I... I'm leaving... I'm leaving...*" His eyes ready to burst, his body convulsing, almost melting from within. I could see nothing around him, but he... He was seeing something, of that I am sure. He backed away blindly, never leaving my eyes, then suddenly spun round, stumbled, struck the door. Looking back I believe my protector was toying with him. He fled swearing under his breath, almost screaming, the door slammed behind him with a violence that shook the walls. And then... Nothing. Only silence. I remained there clutching the jaguar to me, mute, frozen, relieved Pierre was safe. But that silence... It was inhabited. I rushed to the front door and blocked it with the hallway cupboard, adrenaline gave me such strength it took less than a minute. I could have moved a mountain that day. Since then I have asked myself: "*Who stopped him? Who protected us, me and my baby, that afternoon?*" Deep inside I know. That protection, my guardian angel. He always returns, like a golden thread woven through my stories.

Do you think nature
doesn't speak to you ?

My friend, the stone

It was just a stone... But it protected me far more than you would ever believe. When I left my partner, I took my three children, a few wooden crates and the will to be reborn. Words that hurt, gestures that wounded... Enough was enough. I left everything behind. I was chasing peace. I did not need ghosts from the past. We found refuge in a large house in the middle of the woods, with trees, ponds, wild flowers of every colour filling the fields, a whole hectare just for me, my children... And my Nina, a bull terrier I had adopted. Can you imagine? Me, who loves water and wild flowers, I thought: "*Here we'll be fine... This is paradise.*" With a few crates, some salvaged bits and my upholsterer's workshop, I was ready to start from scratch. People even called me "*the woman with the crates.*" But the artist in me found my shelves a little bare and bland, even with the bouquets I picked each morning and placed in vases. So I went walking in the woods in search of something to create with... A stump, a branch, anything at all that might spark some joy. The wind made the leaves sing above me, the ground was soft, still damp with dew, my hands rummaged through the ferns, searching for a piece of wood shaped by time. I loved those moments, sheltered from everything, it felt as if the forest were breathing with me, I felt alone in the world... And yet not quite. And then... I stumbled on something. I fell flat in the mud... The fall of the century! I grumbled the way I know so well. Looking down, I saw a huge stone. Smooth all over, soft as the skin of a pebble. It had tripped me! Staring at it I said: "*You and I didn't start off well... But if you made me notice you, perhaps there's a reason?!*" Determined, I brought it home. Covered in mud, lying among the ferns, it looked like an old clumsy friend. On the way back I spoke to it... As one speaks to a companion. Strange to you, perhaps... But natural to me. Once at the house I set it down by the door and laughing I said: "*Ohhh Youuu, my StoOone, my FrieeenD... You'll WaaaRn Meee When*

SomeBooody CoooMees." Yes, I know what one might think! The next day I heard a noise, a scraping sound like a rasp on the tiles. I went to look... No one. I thought it was a draught. But a few minutes later my mother arrived. She came in and we had coffee. I laughed as I told her of my strange discovery: "*My stone warned me you were coming!*" She laughed... At my childish side, or perhaps... At my gentle madness. The following day, the same noise. That rasping again. This time it was the neighbour, asking for some eggs. And then again... A slower, deeper rubbing. The owner's brother had come to check on us. Each sound... And then a visit. I laughed, but deep down, I began to believe. And then one day the sound came back, but this time it froze my blood. I felt something was wrong. I did not hesitate. I trusted my instinct and my stone. I closed everything: curtains, locks, doors. I hid with the children in the back room. Absolute silence. Minutes later a car pulled up. He arrived. It was him. My ex. My feeling had been right. And my stone had done its work. He hammered on the door. Shouted. Insisted. I did not give in. I held the children close. We held our breath. Not a sound. Not a move. Time had frozen. I was there, hidden, ready for anything. But him... He did not belong here. And my stone was watching. At last he left, muttering... Insults perhaps, or just the wind. He was no doubt convinced he had the wrong house. He never came back. That day I understood... My stone had warned me, it had protected me, it had heard me. It was only a stone... But it rang true. And sometimes that is all it takes to change the course of a story. Believe it... Or not. That stone was my friend.

When the smell of sulphur

It's never without a reason !

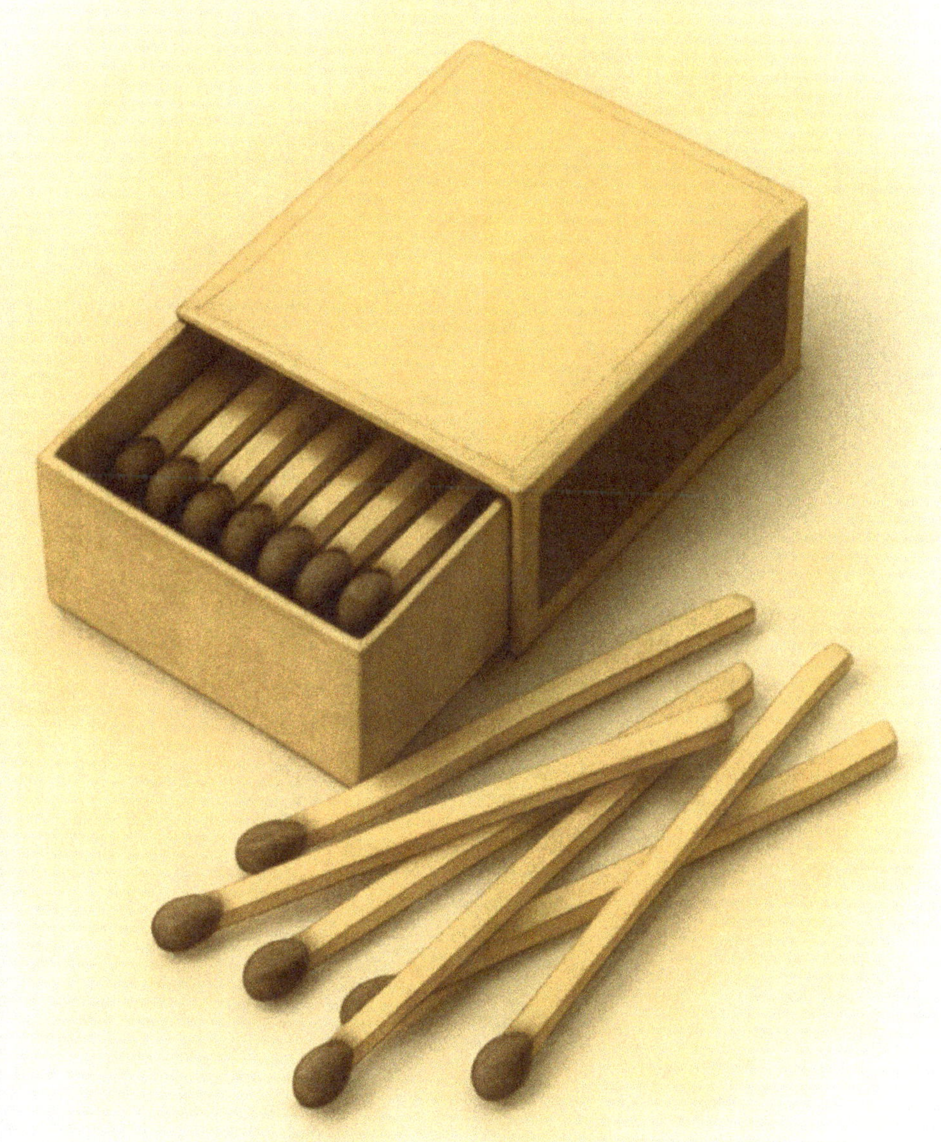

Some houses smell of fire.

Even when nothing is burning, they carry the scent of sulphur. And yet something is heating, the air, the walls, the memories. This house belonged to a friend, Eddy. A vast, majestic dwelling built from thick local stone. It had been wounded by fire, perhaps more than once. A deep scar, cleverly concealed. Eddy offered me his hand at a time when I was alone with my three children. We had no roof above us, only that crushing sense of being invisible to the world. I was on the stage in those days, and Eddy had come to see a play. He heard my story, that I was living in a women's shelter, trying to free myself from the father of my youngest child, to breathe again, to save, to rebuild. That day he wished to help. He invited me to settle on the ground floor. It was beautiful: a park, a pool, flowers everywhere. A dream suspended in mid-air. Eddy drew the gardens by hand. He was a landscape architect, gentle, a dreamer. He would hand me his sketches and I brought them to life. I helped him, and we laughed. But I felt something. The house bore a troubled energy. When I spoke of it, Eddy's face darkened and he told me the story of his former partner. A candle, forgotten, or so she said, though she swore she had blown it out. He had gone to work, and while he was away the house had caught fire. One of those mysteries left unresolved. Three months after we moved in, Eddy fell gravely ill. I chose to help him in return. I went to the hospital every day. And the further I stayed away, the more alive the house seemed, the scent of sulphur clinging to me. One night everything shifted. I had just drifted into sleep when my cat leapt onto my face, claws dug into the sheets, refusing to let go. My daughter was there. We looked at one another. Silent. Then we heard it, cries, howls from the floor above. Broken voices, as if burning through the walls. Souls on fire. I whispered to my daughter: "*It's madness... It sounds like people burning, screaming, seeking the light, begging for help... Do you hear them?*" She looked back at me in silence. She had heard them too. That night we fell asleep huddled together, hearts pounding, thoughts scattered. Days later I was driving with my mother. Barely eight hundred metres along the road I said: "*I smell fire, Mum... This isn't right.*" She turned at once. I ran into the house. A bitter smell struck my throat. Smoke seeped from a wall. An old cable, long forgotten, had begun heating the plasterboard just below the ceiling. I cut the power, secured the wires, and sat on the wide staircase in the hush of my thoughts, recalling the story of the candle. There were no flames, not this time. My instinct, or rather that persistent smell of fire, had warned me. And I was right to heed it. In a village, news spreads fast. A few days later an elderly man from nearby came to see me. I welcomed him with coffee. Without meeting my eyes, embarrassed perhaps at how I might respond, he murmured: "*You know, there are things one does not say to just anyone.*" And then he confided: "*I was a boy when my mother told me that before, it had been a farm. It burned quicker than the flames of hell... The farmers, the animals, everything was consumed...That house is cursed...And if I may offer you advice, my dear lady, leave this place... Take your children. Do not wait too long.*" And in that instant, I understood. The candle, she swore she had extinguished it. The cable, ready to set the ceiling ablaze. The farm, reduced to ashes. The fear, the sulphur, the screams. It had all been there, for years. Eddy knew... He carried it in his silences, in his sorrowed smiles. He had invited me there in spite of it all. He loved that house so dearly. It bore a cry, one that still echoes. But it was not that cry which drove me away... That cry, I heard it, and I learned to live with it. I spoke to the souls in torment. I told them we could hear them, that we meant no harm. And though the nights were restless and the screams never ceased, I stayed... It was another visitor, darker still, who finally forced me out.

To all Mothers, from
here or elsewhere...
You are never far
from our Hearts...

My mother and the little bell

I went to a well-known flea market in Belgium. Not far from there, there's a hill with a lion on top! While rummaging around, as I always do, I came face-to-face with a little bell a lovely one, with a charming wooden handle. When you're obsessed with certain objects like I am... Well, let's just say I didn't fall far from the tree! I used to go treasure-hunting with my grandmother in flea markets and second-hand shops. Bells, 1920s trinkets, trays, suitcases... I always fall for them. So I brought my little bell home. I polished it, decorated it, and placed it proudly among the crates I use as furniture. Years later, when my mum passed on... I wanted her to take something with her that truly meant a lot to me. A flash my bell! As I gently placed it in her hands, I whispered in her ear: "*Take good care of it on your journey... And if ever there's danger or something odd... Give me a sign, will you?*" Time went by... Until one day, half-asleep, I heard a sharp sound: the clear ring of my bell. At first I thought I was dreaming. Had I really heard it? But yes... It was real. Ten minutes later, an old friend rang my doorbell. We sat down with a bowl of coffee a good rousta, as we say around here! And there, as cool as you like, he offered me a "*financial plan*". Right away, I thought of the bell's warning. My nose told me: "*Watch out, Gaby. This smells like a trap!*" After all that time without news... Why suddenly come back with that kind of idea? I politely declined. Two weeks later, I saw in the newspaper: he'd been part of a scam. That's when I understood: my mother had warned me. And it wasn't the last time. During some roadworks near my house, I had asked the contractor to remove part of my fence. As I was going to pay him... Ding! My bell again. I turned around, grabbed my phone, and recorded the conversation. Just in case! And thank goodness I did. A few days later, the boss came banging on my door furious demanding more money. Thanks to the recording, I was able to prove my good faith.

He left somewhat calmer… With a little idea brewing in the back of his mind, I'd say. And me? I knew: my mum had been looking out for me. Again. From that day on, I've known that this bell isn't just a memory. It's a connection. A bridge between her and me. If she's allowed, she warns me. But some things… We have to go through. Up there, they can't always step in when they'd like to. Sometimes they send a sign. Sometimes, they just watch… And let us learn. From time to time… She comes back in other ways. In a vivid dream. Or I feel the weight of her presence settling gently at the edge of the bed. When I write, sometimes… I feel her. Her handwriting… It's her. Like a wink on the page. Even from over there, she's still by my side. I love you, Mum. But that… The way she shows up… I'll tell you about it another time.

When shadows take shape...
Beware !

The small man in black

At the time, I was living in a huge, beautiful house surrounded by ponds and wild plants, with my three children. I've already told you about that house. The one that smelled of fire. But it wasn't that strange smell that made me leave. No. What truly made me run away... Was what happened that night. The night was very calm. I was asleep in my big bed. My sleep was light I couldn't get used to the noises of the house... Until suddenly, I was jolted awake by a presence pinning my face to the side. With indescribable strength. I couldn't move. I was frozen. My heart started pounding like mad. I was paralysed. Then, an icy voice whispered into my ear, stretching some words like venom: "*If You Want to Liiive... Don't Looook at Me...*" Silence. Then, even closer: "*Listen To Me... Juuust LiSten...*" I was terrified. I didn't try to see his face. I just know he was small, terrifyingly strong, and dressed all in black. He went on murmuring in my neck with that chilling voice: "*I am... DeeaaTh... And... I Don'T LiiiKe Being DisturBed... This House... Is Miiine! I EnjoY My SoliTuuuDe... Go. TaKe Your Brats... And Never CoMe*

Baaack!" At that point, believe me, I got the message. Loud and clear. I was petrified. That place was his refuge, and his alone. I had no business being there. Then he released my face. He walked out of the room, slowly... Clearly pleased with the effect he'd had. As you can imagine, I didn't sleep a wink that night. The next day, I was in the kitchen with my daughter, preparing a meal, when he passed by... As if nothing had happened. Just to remind me that he was real. That I hadn't dreamed it. Seriously? He dares? The nerve! Is he mocking me? How could I ever forget what he put me through? I still hear his venomous voice in my head claiming that place as his, and his alone. A place he defended like a wild animal ready to bite. My daughter and I acted like we hadn't seen him. We went on with our chores, pretending everything was normal. At least, on the surface. It's not that I believe he was there it's a certainty. He was watching us. Feeding on our silent discomfort. After that, from time to time, we'd see him slip by in the hallway... Or flicker past the TV as it lost signal. The screen would go black, as if he was saying: "*I'm here. Now get out.*" His appearances became less frequent once he realised we were packing. He'd probably overheard my mother and me talking about it. A few weeks later, we left the house and moved in with Mum. As we loaded the final box into the truck, I looked back at the front door... And I caught a glimpse of him. Pleased. Victorious. I didn't wait to be told twice. Even now, just talking about it gives me chills. Some places don't belong to us. Sometimes... You just have to go. When the last grain begins to fall, time is running out. As for me... I never saw that little man in black again. And honestly? I'm perfectly fine with that.

By custom and tradition…

Let faith endure.

The blue ring

When I was young, I often went to visit my grandmother. She lived in a caravan, on the same land as me. I was just starting to become a young woman. And with that... Came the pain, the changes... One day, she called me over and said:

"*Come. I've got something for you.*" She took a thick piece of yarn, a blue ring, and tied eight knots... Then, with the ninth... She wrapped the cord around my waist, whispering a prayer to a Saint. And she said: "*Keep this close. You might need it one day... You never know!*" Years later... I was twenty, pregnant with my son Pierre. But at four months, complications began. The doctor wanted to terminate the pregnancy. I refused. Flat out. I stayed in the hospital for a week, lying down, holding on. But when I returned to work, the tram rides, the stress... Everything started again. Back to the hospital! And there the same doctor, with the same tone, weary and smug, greeted me and said coldly: "*This pregnancy won't last. You have to decide.*" I looked at him with a little smile and said: "*I've got a remedy.*" He stared at me... And laughed. A cold, mocking laugh. But I knew. Once home, I asked my partner to find me a blue ring. Poor guy he searched all over Brussels! After a long hunt, he found one. I tied it around my waist,

just like my grandmother had taught me. One... Two... Nine knots! The months passed. And Pierre was born, healthy and strong. The next day, in the shower, the cord came loose... The ring snapped clean and hit the shower tray with a loud crack. As if I no longer needed it. I thought of my grandmother.
And I thanked her for that beautiful gift.

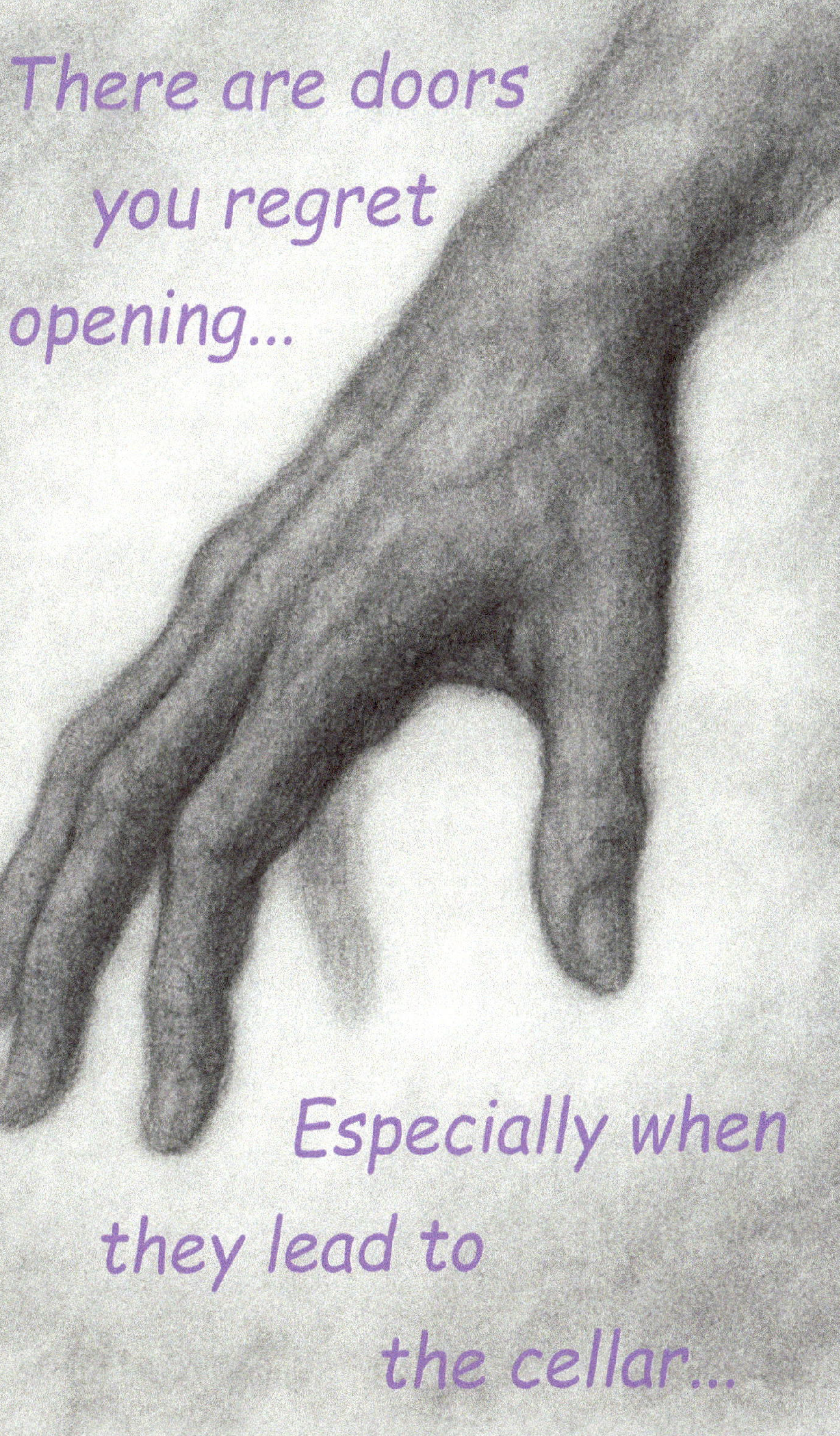
There are doors
you regret
opening...
Especially when
they lead to
the cellar...

That strange mansion

At the time, I was working as a housekeeper in an old mansion. A place completely frozen in time... And in that mansion, there was this hallway. The one on the first floor. Every time I walked through it alone, something inexplicable would happen. An invisible force would literally throw me to the floor. Not just a clumsy fall. No. It was violent... As if someone or something had shoved me hard. My things flew all around me. And I couldn't move. Paralysed by a presence I couldn't see. I'd stay there, stuck... As if the walls themselves had swallowed me. At first, I thought, maybe it's in my head. Some might call it "hallucination", "psychosis"... Yeah right! And if it was in my head, well, then my head went and rented the downstairs floor to a ghost! But no. It was real. Too real. Then one day, I went down to the basement. I had some tidying up to do. A dusty old cabinet was blocking the back wall. I decided to push it aside. And there, just behind it... I discovered an old well. Covered by a huge slab of concrete. And on that slab... a cross. But not just any cross. An upside-down one. A freezing chill shot down my spine. And around my neck... I felt a gust of air. Icy cold. Like an invisible hand brushing against my skin. And for me, cold like that is never a good sign. I bolted back upstairs, not looking back once. But something inside me refused to leave it like that. I was terrified... But I knew I had to act. So I grabbed a crucifix and some salt. Then back down I went, trembling like a leaf... But I went. I placed the cross. I scattered salt all around the well. I started praying. And then... Everything cut out. Darkness. Total black. I won't lie I panicked. But I guess you already figured that part out. I ran up those stairs like my life depended on it four steps at a time and I never dared to look back. I was too afraid of what I might see. And then... Silence. Calm. From that day on, I was never thrown to the ground again. Never. But I'd be lying if I said everything was gone. I could still feel a chill brushing over my skin in certain places. Especially in that infamous hallway upstairs. It wasn't exactly fear... more like a disturbance. A kind of shift in the air. Like something was suspended there. Waiting. Watching. Sometimes it felt like someone had just walked right past me without a sound, without a trace, but absolutely present. The walls seemed to listen. The doorknobs always cold. And that damn corridor... It didn't just feel spooky. It swallowed silence. Like it was waiting for something. Or someone. Later on, I started asking around. I needed to understand. And people from the village began to talk. They said that strange ceremonies had taken place in the mansion. Rituals whispered half out loud. Some former staff admitted they had seen things... But no one dared speak about it back then. They kept quiet to protect their jobs... Or maybe out of fear. But the walls... They remembered. And one day, it happened.

A man hanged himself there. A man they all described as kind, happily married, a good father... At least, that's what they said. Some claim he took his own life. Others... That he had help. But no one ever really talked about it. Just vague glances. Tight-lipped silence. A few months later... I left that mansion. Moved on. I never spoke of it again. Except here, of course... But hey. That doesn't count, right? You're not gonna rat me out to the ghosts, are you?

On the other side

A light awaited her...

The white bird

It was summer. I was on holiday in the South with Pierre. He has a converted van. Pierre knows my tastes. He had suggested a few weeks of holiday to clear my mind. So we settled near a river... And there I was, feet in the water. What more could I ask for?

That day, we had prepared a little barbecue. I was bringing the salad when the phone started ringing... On the line, they told me that my mother was seriously ill. That I had to come back. No need to tell me twice. Without hesitation, we hit the road. We were driving fast. Very fast. I watched the trees rushing by, one after the other, without really seeing them. The sky seemed wider than usual. Everything felt suspended, as if the world was holding its breath. The sun was beating down hard, flooding the cabin with light. So I pulled a blanket over my head. It made Pierre smile. And I closed my eyes. I meditated... I asked the universe to be near her... Then I projected a golden light. Soft. Calm. I called my mother. And in that light... I found myself by her side. Just for a moment. She did not speak. But she was there. And so was I. It was as if I had teleported, just to be close to her. There was a kind of flash. And I was back in the cabin. Then a bird appeared. A graceful flight, as if in slow motion... It flew so close to me. Barely a metre away. Right by my side of the window, which was half open. It stayed there for a long time, accompanying us. It was surprising... Almost unreal. A bird flying so close, for so long... As if it knew... As if it had a role to play. A messenger, perhaps. "Look, Pierre, this bird is following us...!" And suddenly, it changed direction. It crossed from my side to his. And at that precise moment, the phone rang again... Mum had gone... Not alone. Not really far. Just to the other side... Of that golden light. And perhaps the bird too... Had crossed to the other side.

[illegible]ed, just to be close to her. There was a kind of flash, and I was back in the cabin. Then a bird appeared. A graceful flight, as if in slow motion. It flew so close to me, barely a metre away. Right by my side of the window, which was half open. I stayed there for a long time, accompanying [illegible]

[illegible]

perhaps, "Look there, this bird is following [illegible]

[illegible]

hold [illegible] tree [illegible] Or the garden [illegible] perhaps the bird [illegible] other side.

Steeep
right up...
GABY
YOUR FORTUNE

My cards

I am a psychic card reader.
I don't read the cards like they do in books.
I lay them out as I feel, in the moment.
From what I sense, right then, right there.
I don't do rituals.
I simply ask for silence.
And I let myself go.
I see...
I sense...
I hear...
Like a piece of music...
I welcome the notes.
And sometimes... A story appears.
Clear. Powerful. Unexpected.
The very one the person came to find. Even without knowing it.

[illegible]

I am a psychic card reader

I don't read the cards like they do in books [illegible]

I lay them out as I feel at the moment

From what I sense right then, right there

I [illegible]

[illegible]

And [illegible]

I see

I sense

[illegible]

I [illegible] the cards

And sometimes [illegible]

Clear, Powerful, Unexpected

The very one the person came to find out [illegible]

without knowing it

A family story

A couple came to see me… Someone had told them about me. They hadn't said much at first, but as the cards began to fall, something revealed itself. A quiet ache. A hollow space… The longing for a child.

She was gentle, calm... You could feel it she carried that hope deep inside her. He, on the other hand, wasn't open at all. Very sceptical. He looked at me like I was there to sell him hope in a bottle. I never take offence. People come with their pasts, their fears, their wounds. I do what I can. I offer my hand. And often, I manage to open a warm space... Where even the most guarded end up laying down a piece of their armour. They had been told their chances were slim. Very slim. But I saw something else. I saw child energy. Not just one! No... Several children in the house. And so much laughter. When I told them this, they looked surprised... But said nothing. So I continued. "*You're going to travel far. And during that trip... Something will spark. A little girl. She's waiting for you.*" "*Have you ever considered adoption?*" The husband cut in. Firm. Dismissive. Adoption wasn't an option. Full stop. He slammed the door, and the session ended there. But a week later, she called me. She wanted to continue. She said, "*Can we pick up where we left off?*" I smiled. "*You'll see... He'll come around. And when the time is right, he'll love that little girl as if he had carried her himself.*" She left full of hope. Time went by... Five years later, I received a letter. They had adopted a little girl. And she was beautiful. It had been love at first sight. And one day, they would tell her the story... Of the woman with the cards. But the letter didn't stop there. No... Because a few months later, life brought them twins. Two healthy baby boys. A big, beautiful family against all odds had come into being. At the end of the letter, there were two signatures. Including his. And one final line: "*Without you, we would never have considered adoption.*

Thanks to you, we are happy." I read that letter many times. And with my soft little chocolate heart… I cried. But this time… They were tears of joy. What if life sometimes found paths that reason wouldn't even dare imagine?

We crossed paths

Her name was Isabelle. A young woman, lost caught in the grip of addiction. After the death of someone dear to her, she'd fallen in with the wrong crowd. Her eyes were searching for something... Or someone.

When she came to see me, she didn't believe in anything anymore. But I looked at her and I saw. I saw an accident. A shock. Something that would force her to stop everything. To wake up. I told her it wouldn't be easy... But it could be a turning point. I spoke to her about a forgotten passion. Horses. Yes horses. Their strength, their honesty. I didn't know why... But I knew it was the right path. A few months later, the accident came. She survived. Hurt, shaken... But alive. And then, she remembered. My words. That image I had shared with her. She left the country. Found a small riding school. And there... Something opened. The horses welcomed her. They helped her heal. Regain her strength. Rebuild her confidence. Today, Isabelle is no longer trapped in addiction. She lives among horses. And in her eyes... That light has returned. The one she thought she'd lost. Sometimes, a single word is enough to plant a seed. And when the soil is right... That seed becomes a whole new life.

Her father appeared

Annick, curious and a little nervous, had booked a session with me after a friend's recommendation. She sat in her living room, adjusting her camera for an online reading. I welcomed her with a calm smile and began laying out my cards. The air was charged with expectation. Annick felt both excited and anxious about what might unfold. The session began gently. I shared pieces of her life with a precision that, I could see in her eyes, touched her deeply. But then, something unexpected happened. Her camera flickered and a strange shape appeared on screen. At first, it looked like a shifting mosaic. Blurry. Almost unreal. Her heart raced. Fear flashed through her like lightning. She froze, breath caught, as the image grew sharper. It was the face of a man she knew well. In a soft, reassuring voice, I said: "*Don't worry. It's a kind spirit.*" Still trembling, Annick recognised her father who had passed away just a few months earlier. I explained that he had seen her sadness... And had found a way to come through. As if he'd been waiting for this very moment. A wave of emotion crashed over her sorrow and comfort, all at once. With tears in her eyes, she thanked me. And me... Deeply moved, I cried with her. We cried together. Touched by that loving presence. Her father's visit, though brief, brought her a kind of peace she hadn't expected. And even for me, used to these subtle encounters... I must admit, I'm still amazed when a soul appears so clearly. So I understand how overwhelming it must feel for someone who's never seen such a thing. Because yes... That's exactly what happened here: a soul came through. The session ended on a soft note of hope and connection leaving Annick with a serenity she hadn't felt in a very long time. The camera turned off. But her father's message... Stayed with her. Etched in her heart.

The little girl with the kick

It happened during a live session. A young woman was waiting until finally, it was her turn... She gave me her first name and instantly, I felt a deep wound. But I remained quiet. The rule of the live session is: wait for the question. She wanted to know about her love life, her relationship...
A classic. Love always comes up. But then,

I felt pulled in another direction. I asked her, "*You're not from here, are you?*" She smiled and confirmed her origins. So I said, "*There's something dear to your heart that's still over there...*" She answered negatively. I gently insisted and told her it was part of her... And then... I got kicked in the leg! Startled, I looked down: a small silhouette... A little girl, maybe four years old. I said it out loud, right there in the live session, "*Hey! I just got kicked in the leg by a tiny little girl! She's full of energy, that one! A boisterous little girl... Does that ring a bell to anyone?*" Then I added, "*Could she be your sister?*" And that's when it clicked. The young woman gasped and explained: it was her twin sister. She had passed away. She was buried back in their home country. Her parents hadn't had a choice when they moved to Europe. She had been a restless child, always moving. And that kick? *"Totally her style!"* she said. The live session... And the two of us... Were filled with emotion. Silence settled in. We took a moment to breathe. She said she regretted never knowing her. But the little one had simply come to say hello. Maybe to show her that nothing truly ends. That there's a thread that continues.

I remember... There was another soul waiting that day... Mr Remy... He had been patiently waiting his turn. But when he saw the little girl bursting in, he let her go first. Later, his sister, who was also watching the reading, told me, "*That's so him... Always letting others go first.*" A simple recognition. But deeply moving. Even over there... He was still the same.

Soon they'll need a ticket system like at the bakery!

when colours speak...

My colors

I don't choose them. They come.
They impose themselves, like silent obviousness.
They whisper, they vibrate, they guide me.
I perceive them as if I were sheet music...
But instead of notes...
It's colors that settle there.
The colors soak up into me and resonate.
An invisible melody, yet so strong.
All stories, all objects, all people...
Have their own shade, their glow, their whisper.
And maybe you, too, while reading this book, will feel a color rising.
Listen to it. It has something to tell you!

My vision of colors

I start from the principle that in everything a human being, an object, an emotion there is both positive and negative. And it is the same with my colours. "*Being kind is a beautiful quality. But being too kind turns into foolishness. It is no longer kindness.*" "Being *proud can be a flaw... If that pride is used to put others down. But if it helps you lift your head, to remain standing when nothing else holds... Then it becomes a strength."* Come on! Let's take yellow... Just to show you. A square of yellow in a grid of nine colours brings joy, good humour, sometimes a spark of laughter. But too much yellow? And then... We slip. We slide into madness, cunning, deceit. Which only shows... Everything needs balance! Every emotion, every colour, every sensation has its own degree of evolution. Nothing is fixed. Everything vibrates. Everything can grow... Or collapse. A colour is like a flame. It can warm a heart or burn everything in its path. It is not the colour that is bright or destructive... It is what we choose to make of it. Sometimes it caresses you... Sometimes it tears you apart. All colours speak to me. They have their voice, their mood, their way of resonating. They know how to cross through me without warning. I could say so much about each of them. But here, this is not the place. Because colours, in their deep language, deserve a book of their own where they may tell their stories. And believe me... I am working on it. Where every shade tells a tale. A special tool for those who wish to go further.

The writer

I had gone to help a friend. On the terrace, I was drinking my coffee. A pause. A bubble. And then... There was this man. Short, stocky, a little faded, sitting right beside me with his tea. He looked so lonely. So sad. I struck up a conversation. He introduced himself and opened up almost at once. He said he was lost. Uneasy in his own skin. Confused. He couldn't seem to find his path. I wanted to help him. But it's not easy to drop that sort of thing on people without sounding mad. Still... I went for it. I offered to take a look at his future. Or rather, for us to look together at the path he might take. I didn't have my cards with me, but for a square of colours, a piece of paper and a pen would do. Surprised, he agreed. So I picked up a pen and a sheet and said: "*Project nine colours. One at a time.*" He did. I wrote. I observed. I felt. And then I told him what I saw: "*You have a gift for writing. You carry inside you a subject you're passionate about... But you lack confidence because someone put you down. Broke you. Humiliated you. Someone close. Someone you trusted completely.*" His face changed. A tear slid down. He listened more closely. "*There is a subject you've carried*

for years, but your lack of confidence paralyses you... And that's such a shame. Because you've got gold at the tip of your pen."
He was shaken. He spoke of his mother, who had always told him he was useless at everything. He told me a bit about his studies, his depression... And that he had always dreamt of writing. We talked about chance. A cancelled appointment for him and there he was, on that terrace he would never have gone to otherwise. And me, that day, helping a friend when I was meant to be in Brussels. Two paths that never should have crossed. And yet... There we were. He and I. I heard from him recently. He's on his fifth book now. Happier than ever.
Even his mother had to admit at last: "he was born for this."

Green hands

Sophie was in her forties. Curious, she had booked an appointment. She wanted to try the nine-colour grid. On the day, we met by video call. She told me she was at a crossroads. Her job, the endless work-sleep-repeat routine...

That was over. She knew there was "*something else*", but couldn't see what. So I explained the principle. She projected the colours to me, one by one. I wrote them down. I felt them. The colours settled within me like notes on a music sheet. And then... What struck me was the video image itself. A green background, and her hands... They were green. It was obvious. I told her: "*You have a gift. The gift of healing.*" She insisted on orange... Sky blue... That confirmed what I was sensing. I saw her grandmother always there, by her side. A magnetiser, a well-known healer, who had passed on her prayer. Sophie was delighted that her grandmother appeared in her grid of colours. She told me about the courses she had taken, because she liked diplomas. "It looks more serious," she said. But I could see she already knew. She carried it all within her. The courses were superfluous. Yet, if they reassured her... Why not. Her husband preferred discretion. He didn't like to "draw attention to himself", and wished she wouldn't either. So, for years, she put all that aside. She forgot that part of herself. She settled for what he wanted. For what was expected of her. But that fire... It cannot be extinguished! I told her choices were approaching. Decisions. A turning point. Renewal was coming. The following year, she moved out. She left everything behind... And opened a small practice at home. Sometimes she heals remotely, when people reach out to her. Today, she is happy to "be Herself."

My little chocolate heart for a world both tender and cruel

My early childhood

There are silent moments...

When something opens. Drawn to details...

That speak volumes.

A wider gaze.

An early lucidity.

Two awakenings... Two jolts...

And everything shifts.

The world was already signalling to me...

I understood without knowing how to explain.

Those sparks of awakening shaped...

The woman I have become.

At the grand age of six

The day I knew... As a child, they used to say I was special. Different. With a frank, piercing gaze... clumsy, cheeky... And a tiny chocolate heart for my sensitivity. Quite a cocktail! At six years old, I was living what looked like an ordinary day, full of laughter and joy, surrounded by my cousins. My favourite aunt the one I loved to tell everything to had come to spend the day with us. I adored her. She was hilarious. She had the gift of turning any tale into a burst of laughter. The sun was shining, the barbecue crackling, and everyone was enjoying themselves in the garden. Mum let me stay with the grown-ups, provided I kept quiet. So I sat there, discreet, observing. My curiosity absorbed every detail of that summer's day. As dusk began to fall, it was time for my Auntie to head home. In a soft yet firm voice, I took her hand and said: "*No, Auntie... You mustn't leave now. Leave later. The road isn't good right now.*" My parents exchanged an awkward glance. It wasn't exactly the sort of remark one expects at such a moment. But my Auntie, intrigued by my seriousness, decided to stay a while longer. She listened to me. In our family, it's passed down from mother to

daughter: when an intuition comes, you listen. You never know. The hours went by, filled with laughter and play. Later, she finally set off. On the way back, she discovered there had been a terrible accident on the motorway. The radio announced the traffic had been blocked for at least two hours. A chill ran through her. She realised that if she had left earlier, she would have been caught right in the middle of it. The next day, she called Mum to tell her about the journey home and said: "*If I hadn't listened to the little one... I might not even be here to tell you this!*" That day, something shifted in the family. My reputation began to take shape. But for me, it had simply begun with a warning to my funny aunt.
That was my very first memory.

At the grand age of ten

We had just left the caravan. Now we were living in a huge house that Mum and Dad had built on the land Grandma had given us. It was big, it was beautiful... And I felt a bit like a princess. In the evenings, Dad watched the news. That was his time. No one was to speak during the broadcast. So we all sat there, gathered around the television. On the screen, there was a report. Children in Africa. They said they were starving. I didn't understand... I was ten years old. I saw a little boy with a swollen belly. So I asked Mum: "*But... why is his belly like that if he hasn't eaten? That's not possible. He must have eaten, surely?*" And in my head, I heard the song we used to sing at school: "*My tummy's tight and full... thank you, dear Jesus!*" Mum looked at me and explained that when someone is starving, the belly can swell. It's the body's reaction. And in that instant, I felt a sharp pang. I looked at the little boy and wanted to cry for him.

But right after that, there was another report. A man stepped off a plane. He wore rings on every finger, a golden staff, glittering clothes, necklaces upon necklaces. He looked like a king. Or a magician! I turned to Mum and said: "*Mum... That's not kind... That's not fair. He's so rich... He talks of love and sharing... But he keeps all his gold! And that little boy is hungry? Why doesn't he give him his jewels?"* Mum looked at me and said: "*Oh, my little Trinette, that's the world. That's how people in power are."* I said nothing. I just kept watching the screen. But in my head, everything tangled. I had understood something... Or perhaps I had lost a piece of innocence. I don't know. But from that year on... I never saw the world in the same way again. At ten years old, I didn't yet have the words. I just felt that something was wrong. I held two images in my mind... That starving child, and that man who sparkled. They collided within me. And from that day on, my gaze was different. I have never understood how someone can laugh whilst another weeps. I have never understood how one could become one-armed... Instead of reaching out a hand. That day, I think I realised that the world is not always fair.

m[illegible] talks of love and sharing. But he keeps all the gold! And that little boy is hungry! Why doesn't he give him his jewels?" Mum looked at me and said, "Oh! [illegible] [illegible] the world. That's how people in power are." I said nothing. I just kept watching the screen, but in my head, everything tangled. I had [illegible] and [illegible] [illegible].

[illegible]

[illegible] the same [illegible], ten years old. I didn't [illegible] just felt that something [illegible]

[illegible]

[illegible] is different. I [illegible] never understood how someone can [illegible] another way. I've never understood how one could become [illegible]. Instead [illegible] out a [illegible] that day, I think I realised that the world is not always fair.

Astral travel

Astral travel

When the body falls silent...

The soul begins to speak.

All it takes is a suspended moment.

A night when one believes they are asleep...

For everything to shift. It is not a dream.

Not a delusion. It is a departure.

Towards an elsewhere.

To that place where the astral reveals...

That all is connected.

Where there is no more me, no more you...

Only unity within the vastness of the universe.

A journey unlike any other.

A journey never to be forgotten.

A journey unlike any other

After an operation, my bed became my refuge... And silence my only companion. I spent entire days lying still, no movement, no sound... A soft prison, imposed by a body worn out and aching. That evening I fell asleep on my back, which I never do. I hate it. It always startles me awake, and it frightens me. But this time I had no choice. I was stuck, so I let go or so I thought. I slipped into what I believed was sleep. But that night it was something else. A heavy pressure weighed upon me, as if I were sinking into the mattress, drawn into the depths. Then I felt myself slip, like a leaf being gently pulled from its envelope. And there I was another me, a double. The first thing I saw was a cord: a glowing thread, like a vine of energy, still tying me to my earthly shell. I saw my face, pale, exhausted, marked by pain. But strangely I felt nothing. I was elsewhere detached, light, fascinated. The world around me had changed. Light shone from everything, as if it came from within the objects themselves. Colours were warmer, more vivid than anything on earth. It was breathtaking. Magical. I turned and my face passed through the closed curtains. There I saw the sky a starry sky so close I could touch it. No, more than that. I was one with it. I let myself drift in that sensation. I visited my flat, the home where I lived with my three children. One by one, I hovered above them. They were sleeping peacefully, so I let them dream and continued my journey. The strangest part? I didn't need to open doors. I passed through walls, as if the bricks and I were one. The universe and I were one. No body, no limits, no borders. I drifted down to the lower floors. At the entrance door, I heard a voice calling me. In an instant, still tethered by that luminous cord, I returned to my suffering body reluctantly. I opened my eyes and told my partner everything. He understood nothing. But I knew. I had taken a magnificent journey between two worlds. Up there, I had been allowed to consciously discover another space... Astral Travel.

A thread between two worlds

I've taken other conscious journeys since then. Most of us do... Without even realising it. There are different planes. Different realms. And depending on our level what we can bear, what we're ready to understand we visit one or another. There is a realm that hurts... You wander through it among lost souls. You feel their pain, their drifting. Another realm can be frightening. There, the souls are hard to look at. Ugly, yes... But more in what they radiate. In those moments, you must stay calm. Do not answer. Do not react. Do not give them your attention. And then... There are other realms. Higher ones. Places of learning. Realms where knowledge is shared. Sometimes you return with insights you did not have when you left. Whatever the place, there is always that link. That cord. That golden thread tying us to our body, to the earthly plane. And all it takes is the will… To return.

Life has
no end...
Each life is
a stopover

Reincarnation

There are encounters that shake us...
Sensations that come from afar.
We believe we come into the world only once.
But sometimes, certain faces or certain places unsettle us.
As if something within us already knew.
A glance, a fear, a sensation, a scent...
Like an echo from the past.
And what if we came back?
Not to redo, but to understand.
To love a little better.
To heal... Maybe each life is a chance...
A gift to the soul...
Not a repetition, but another version of oneself.
A continuation, a stopover, a new breath.
And when it vibrates strongly, deep inside,
Perhaps it is memory stirring.

A shaman, a vision, a life

I don't often tell this story. Because honestly... I never know how to bring it up. It's the kind of tale you lock away in a chest of strange memories, somewhere between "you have to live it to believe it" and "they'll just think I've lost the plot." And yet, it happened! Looking back...

it shook me to my core. My mother had advised me to meet a shaman. So I went. It was winter... snow was falling heavily. I remember it well: I wore a thick black turtleneck, pulled up high. Nothing, absolutely nothing, visible. The shaman and I settled in comfortably. Then she began to speak of my past lives. The first she mentioned was on the continent of Mu. You know, that vanished civilisation, a little like Atlantis. But in Mu, there were artists, craftsmen, people who moved things forward. And then she described me: "You created... You dyed fabrics, made decorations. But above all... you shared your knowledge." I stared at her, a bit stunned. Because what she couldn't possibly know was that for seven years already, I'd been upholstering. That I dyed my own fabrics. That my mother had passed on some basics to me... And at that very moment, I was right in the middle of it. After supporting a friend through illness, after his passing, after keeping the house and the children going... I had decided to take my life back into my own hands. I had moved to a small town, and three days before meeting the shaman, I had found a house with a workshop. My future workshop. And then she carried on. She told me I had innate gifts, very ancient ones. She saw me as a powerful witch, known and feared. One day, a cruel king had wanted me to work for him. He craved my powers to harm his enemies. At first, I agreed, prepared potions. Then, realising how far he wanted to go, I refused. He threatened me. My family, my children... I was trapped. So, she said, I let myself be swallowed by black magic. Until the moment I said stop. And so, the king took revenge. He had my loved ones massacred. And since I still refused to give in, he had me drawn and quartered in the middle of a public square, before the whole crowd. I stared at her, frozen. Because in this life, I suffer from a condition that makes my joints dislocate easily. And I have two long scars on my arms. Strange scars. The kind said to be traces visible from a past life. I pulled down my turtleneck. She turned pale... She told me: "This is the first time I've had such obvious proof, right there, before my eyes." The very next day, I opened my workshop to live my passion... and to give classes too. What I felt that day was like a fog. A mix of dizziness, alignment and questions. This story is not one I control. I don't even always know if I should believe it... Or simply keep it as a wink from destiny. But what I do know, even when we can never be sure... is that there are no coincidences. That every person I crossed paths with, every bit of knowledge rediscovered, the gestures, the memories—everything was there to remind me. Of who I was. Of what I already knew... Well then, it's time to close the grimoire... But stay close by...

you never know what the next chapter might bring.

Notes from elsewhere

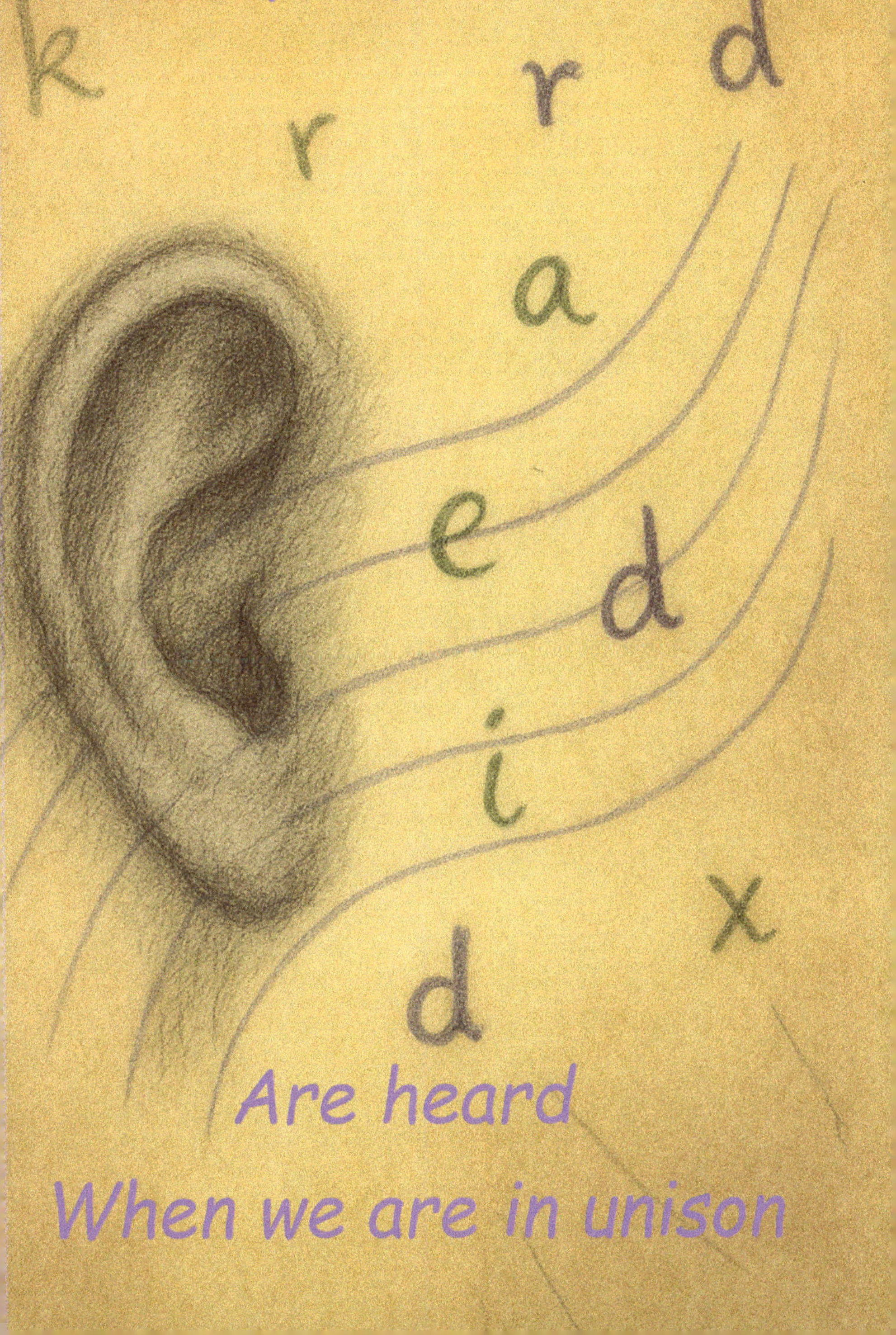

Are heard

When we are in unison

That voice I hear

Between the visible worlds

and the others,

where there is vibration,

there is a breath.

It crosses the silence.

It comes without warning.

That voice has always been with me.

It is not a dream, nor a thought...

It is a discreet, benevolent presence...

Sometimes I listen.

Sometimes I ignore it.

But it is always there.

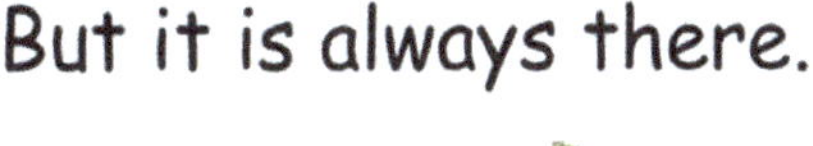

The voice [illegible]

Between the visible world

and the others,

where there is vibration

there is no breath.

[illegible]

[illegible] without [illegible]

That voice has always been with me.

It is not a dream, nor a thought

[illegible]

[illegible]

Sometimes I [illegible]

[illegible]

My voice

People might think I'm rambling. That my mind is racing. But for as long as I can remember, there has been a voice. Not a voice like a memory, not a voice of madness either. A presence. A certainty. It does not speak much. It whispers, it breathes. Sometimes just a word. An intuition that imposes itself.

A vibration that slides into my head. As if to say: "*Be careful.*" "*Not that way.*" "*Look.*" ... I do not know who it is. I call it my voice. Perhaps my guardian angel. Perhaps my double from elsewhere... I do not know. But what I do know is that every time I listened to it, something essential happened. A danger avoided, or a precious moment that would not have existed without it. And it has also happened that I did not listen... To my great regret.

And then... There is the shadow one

I have often spoken of that voice that helps me, the one that lights my path.
But there is another that believes it rules the place. It thinks I belong to it... Which is far from true. My soul is not for sale. It pretends to know me... Luring me with the mirage of an oasis. A reflection. An empty word disguised as light. But I do not give in. It does not seek to lift me up. It wants to bring me down.
It whispers to mislead me. And sometimes, it screams... Just to make me bend. Darkness devours... Or at least... It tries.
I call it "the other."

[illegible]

I have often spoken of that voice that helps [illegible]

[illegible] me, the one that lights my path.

But there is another that believes, unlike the [illegible]

voice. It thinks I belong to it. Which is fed

from [illegible] is not [illegible] Darkness [illegible]

[illegible]

[illegible]

light. But I do not give in. [illegible]

[illegible]

[illegible]

I [illegible]

The other

It is not mine, ...
It comes from afar.
It wants to build nothing, ...
It breathes doubt.
It pretends to know, ...
It mocks.

It attacks for sport, ...
Hoping I will falter.
It whispers as if I were fragile, ...
Seeking a crack.
It tries to frighten me, ...
Sometimes it screams.
But it has not found one.
I see it... I hear it...
But I do not answer...
It is the other...
And the other...
Means nothing to me.
Dark forces do not cross my soul.

Curtains !

It is time to...

close the Grimoire !

Here is a little of me...

I am neither prophet, nor guide, nor model.
I have never claimed to hold the truth.
I only tell my own...
The idea of this book sprouted through all the questions I was asked.

To shed light on a parallel world.
And to offer a spark to those who seek another vision...
I do not write to convince. But to connect...
One breath to another.
A story from soul to soul...
If these pages have resonated within you, then this book will have served its purpose...

Yours sincerely, Gaby

To continue following my stories:
TikTok (live): @gabylibellule
Facebook: Gaby Libellule
contact:leschroniquesdegaby@hotmail.com
www.leschroniquesdegabylibellule.com

To Guss...

I wish to thank Guss, my faithful cosmic friend, who helped me carry this project through! Our countless bursts of laughter, our verbal ping-pong, our patience with one another...

All wrapped in a bond of complicity like no other!

Gaby Libellule

Table of Contents

Words from you

www.ingramcontent.com/pod-product-compliance
Lightning Source LLC
La Vergne TN
LVHW010831120826
845149LV00016B/763

* 9 7 8 2 9 6 0 3 9 0 8 2 7 *